T0194065

GIRL IN THE MIRROR
REFLECTIONS BY JO

K. J. WEBER

MAY WE SEE THE WORLD WITH GENTLE EYES

WESTBOW
PRESS®
A DIVISION OF THOMAS NELSON
& ZONDERVAN

This book is a work of non-fiction. Unless otherwise noted, the author and the publisher
make no explicit guarantees as to the accuracy of the information contained in this book
and in some cases, names of people and places have been altered to protect their privacy.

WestBow Press books may be ordered through booksellers or by contacting:

WestBow Press
A Division of Thomas Nelson & Zondervan
1663 Liberty Drive
Bloomington, IN 47403
www.westbowpress.com
1 (866) 928-1240

Because of the dynamic nature of the Internet, any web addresses or links contained in
this book may have changed since publication and may no longer be valid. The views
expressed in this work are solely those of the author and do not necessarily reflect the
views of the publisher, and the publisher hereby disclaims any responsibility for them.

Cover Image © Can Stock Photo/lilac
Cover Designer: Madison Dettor

Scripture quotations marked (NLT) are taken from the Holy Bible,
New Living Translation, copyright ©1996, 2004, 2007, 2013, 2015 by
Tyndale House Foundation. Used by permission of Tyndale House
Publishers, Inc., Carol Stream, Illinois 60188. All rights reserved.

Scripture quotations marked (NIV) are taken from the Holy Bible, New
International Version®, NIV®. Copyright © 1973, 1978, 1984, 2011 by Biblica,
Inc.™ Used by permission of Zondervan. All rights reserved worldwide. www.
zondervan.com The "NIV" and "New International Version" are trademarks
registered in the United States Patent and Trademark Office by Biblica, Inc.

ISBN: 978-1-9736-1895-9 (sc)
ISBN: 978-1-9736-1897-3 (hc)
ISBN: 978-1-9736-1896-6 (e)

Library of Congress Control Number: 2018901474

Print information available on the last page.

WestBow Press rev. date: 3/23/2018

KJWeberAuthor.com

To my husband, Chris, who has been my tireless *warrior*, loving me through each day, never letting go of my hand, and assuring me that "tomorrow is going to be a better day." You are my *hero* and my *rock*. I love you.

To the *sunshine of my life*, my beautiful daughter, Casey. I love you. To my mom, who has been an overcomer and great supporter (the one who calls me "honey")—I love you. To my dad (the one who calls me "buddy"), you bring a smile to my face, and I adore you. To my two sisters, Kelly and Karla. Life would be empty without you. To my twin brothers, Ronnie and Bobby, the biggest *surprise* of my life! I love you both. To my friend Rodney, who said I had something to say. To all the people in my life, and to those whom I've never met, who inspired me to write from my heart. Thank you.

And to my *forever friend*, Hosy Lala, who inspired me to write my first poem.

And most of all, to the mighty God who put me on this earth, knowing each day before it came to pass.

CONTENTS

LOVE LETTERS TO FAMILY

FANTASTICAL

INSPIRATIONAL

INTRODUCTION

Life-changing events. Many of us go through them. Sometimes changing the trajectory of our lives. Mine was pain.

It was 1990. I was teaching music in Asheville, North Carolina and had gone to yet another doctor's appointment, something that I had unfortunately grown accustomed to doing. "You're going to have to give up singing," the doctor said. If you don't, you will have deformation and arthritis in your jaw." The diagnosis this time was TMJ (temporomandibular joint syndrome), something a singer never wants to hear. Yes, I could still sing, but I would have to pay the consequences—both in the short term and the future.

I left the doctor's office devastated. I had sung all my life. That's all I had ever wanted to do. And now, someone was telling me that part of my life was over. What was my identity now? My life started spinning. I became deeply depressed, and that affected every aspect of my life. No longer was I the Jo I once knew. I was lost. The other medical diagnoses that had just been given to me fell by the wayside. What was I going to do now? My training was in music. I sang. That's what I did. That was my identity.

Soon I would learn a very important lesson: our identity is in Christ, in Him alone. Singing did not define me. God did. I was complete in Him. Whatever happened in the future was up to me. Would I trust Him? I would always grieve the part of my life I'd spent singing. But God had other plans for me, and it would take me a long time to realize this and place me on many different paths, many painful and lonely ones, and ones I would not have imagined.

I still hurt. In fact, I'm never out of pain. As I said, there were many other diagnoses I was given at the time, and ones that have kept coming through the many years since. I cannot sit here and tell you that my life got easier. It didn't. Every day I ask God to heal me and to give me relief, but that day has not come yet. It may not come until I am in heaven. Until then, I want to have an impact on the world. I will get up every day and keep trying to do what God would have me do.

To be honest, while writing *Girl in the Mirror*, I wanted to leave out the part of my life that is called *chronic pain*—the very reason I am an expert on suffering, empathy, and compassion. I wanted one part of my life *not* to include the phrase *chronic pain*. However, if I am to be authentic, a word that some might say *defines me*, I must not exclude the very reason that I write.

I write for many reasons: to release pain through words; to encourage others; to lament and cry out to the Lord; to express what I see in the world around me; and to let those I love know what they mean to me.

So it is, through this very long and difficult journey, that this book of poetry has come into being. I pray that as you read these poems, they will bring you encouragement, and will stir your heart. I also pray that they will help you to look inside yourself and at the world around you.

As each of us walks through this life, we tend to focus on ourselves and our problems. This book of poetry allows us not only to reflect on our deepest thoughts and emotions but also to realize the beauty inside others, and the amazing world that we were given. It takes you to memories of loved ones and helps you realize what they mean to you. These verses mirror what is going on in our world and show us who is in control, and allow us to celebrate all that is around us as each of us walks down our own path.

REFLECTIONS BY JO

MORE

I want,

I want to be more.

I want to be well.

I want to contribute.

I want to make a difference.

I want to be healthy.

I want to be like I used to be.

I want to be social.

I want to be active.

I want to go out more.

I want to not be different.

I want to wake up without pain.

I want to go to bed without pain.

I want to have *good days.*

I want,

I want more …

IN THE DARKNESS OF THE NIGHT

In the darkness of the night,
I wake up with the hope

that the aching in my body
will have lost its way, not show.

Sometimes I desire
not to return to sleep,

so I can test and see
if the pain has taken leave.

But then I see the need
to wander back to bed.

I lie my weary body
across the soft, warm bed.

If I have a chance,
to make it through the day,

I must keep going back,
though the night, I want to stay.

For, you see, it is in the night
that peace can be found,

with no stimulation
or any kind of sounds.

In the moments of quiet,
while the day has not begun,

my body believes its task
can surely be done.

It gives me a sense
of what I could do.

If pain were not my companion,
the day I could get through.

So I'll try to go to sleep
and rest a little more.

Tomorrow's another day.

I will hope forevermore …

SOMEONE LIKE ME

What do you say to someone like me,
someone like me who seeks to be free.

Someone who wants a life not known,
a day without pain, a day of her own.

What do you say when tears flow down,
when prayers don't come,
not easily found?

What do you say, o Lord, my God,
the One who placed, the stars above

the One who makes the planets turn,
the One whose light will always burn?

What do you say to someone whose soul
is weary from this life and its toll,

whose resting place has lost its way,
whose desperate pleas lie on her face?

Dry up her tears falling down;
the world is not, her resting ground …

NO ONE KNOWS BUT YOU

No one knows but you, O Lord,
the pain inside of me.

No one knows how hard I try
to stay upon my knees.

When I wake and when I sleep,
I come to You and ask,

"Please, dear Lord,
help me now.
The agony must pass."

Draw me near, and give me strength
to make it through today.

For no one knows upon this earth
the world that I must face.

NOT SEEN

You look upon my face today
and ask how I am doing.

Although I look the part outside,
the inside is not showing.

I try to play the part I should
and give you what you seek,

but inside this body of mine
is pain so very deep.

You see, you don't know the way
I suffered through the night,

Or that upon my awakening,
I couldn't see the light.

The pain I took to bed with me
lingers on despite.

And yet I try to go through life
while pain, I always fight.

I want to tell you, "Don't be fooled
by what you see outside."

For every day I carry with me
the pain I have inside.

GIRL IN THE MIRROR

Girl in the mirror,
passing through time.

Unanswered questions,
living a rhyme.

Mind on herself,
though others she did see,

searching and waiting
for something to be.

Purpose all along,
not of choice,

but reaching others
would be her voice.

Not through singing
or other endeavors,

strands of life
seem to go on forever.

Suffering, no joke,
day after day,

letting His hand
guide the way.

Girl in the mirror,
can it be so?

Is this the life
intended

for Jo?

MY DEAR

—

Written from the perspective of God

Is this the life you seek, My dear,
the one to keep and hold you near?

Is this the life you seek, I say,
the one you thought was on its way,

the one you know would keep you meek,
would follow Me, you'd always seek?

Is this the one you had in mind,
or did you have to leave behind

the one you always wished could be,
not the one I planned for thee?

So listen dear, as I speak,
I'm going to give you the life you seek.

Will it be the one you asked?
No, I will give you one that lasts—

lasts beyond the pain you feel,
a life surpassed, a life unreal.

So listen, *dear*, I'll tell you how
the life you seek is here and now.

Reflections by Jo

JO

—

To my Father in heaven

Who is this girl,
this one named Jo,

the one who seeks
to love You so,

the girl whose known You
all the while,

who preached of You
as a child,

the one who sang
her songs of praise

to give her all
in You, remain.

LET IT BE SO

Lord, if it be Your will today,
let this time of suffering be done.

I promise not to forget what I've learned,
so others can be shown

to hold on tightly to
Your hand, which won't let go.

So if it be Your will today,

I say,

"Let it be so."

TODAY

Today, we have a choice
to laugh or cry.

Sometimes we hit bottom
and don't know why.

Each pain unwelcome
but somehow God's plan,

maybe to keep us
close to Him.

Never sure what each hour
will bring,

relying on God
in all things.

Many have walked
the path of pain,

some pass on;
others remain.

Each of us,
a story untold,

keeps searching for God
as our lives unfold ...

WHAT LIES AHEAD

"I don't know what lies ahead,
what upon the earth," she said.

"Life can be full of dread,
but He will give my daily bread."

Fear not what day will bring to pass,
for from the Lord, she must ask.

Her eyes on Him for every task
so say not what, she must ask,

her eyes on Him,
for every task.

So, say not what
she must ask.

DEDICATIONS

ABUSE OF LIFE

Dedicated to those killed by a terrorist attack in Barcelona, Spain
August 17, 2017

What sets us apart?

Is it the beating of our hearts?
Is it the path we were set upon?
Is it the path that went so wrong?

Did we choose to honor mankind,
or devour the light that was to shine?

Are we sharing the same earth,
or did the darkness become our girth?

Did it seep down in our souls,
the light, the gift, He gave us all?

Why the darkness one would choose
instead of shining through and through?

Abuse of life, given to us.

What will it take?

The earth shakes.

A single man can evil plan,

can hurt another on demand.

But in this world, he will not win,

for very soon, God will descend.

Every evil,
every wrong—

the man who chose the wide abyss
will one day stand in awe of this.

The payment for his sins on earth
commands a time of rebirth.

If ne'er he does, commit his ways

the wide abyss
he will be laid.

Abuse of life.

What sets us apart?

The heart of man did divide.

Fret not, weary ones on earth.

The day will come
for our rebirth.

MY COUNTRY, O COUNTRY

My country, O country,

what you mean to me.

Many lives were not spared

to keep us free.

I think of the mountains.

I think of the seas.

I think of the forests

and the beautiful trees.

A country that stands

united and free

like the bow of a boat,

holding firmly to Thee.

PROTECT AND SERVE

Dedicated to our men and women in blue after
the police shootings in Dallas, Texas
July 7, 2016

Protect and serve, a sacred creed
to all those who are in need,

no matter color, race, or creed.
running to danger, while others flee.

They give their lives so we can be
a country safe, a country free.

Who is this one, so brave and true,
the one who wears the color blue?

So as a nation mourns our loss,
today we reflect on all we've lost.

Put aside division and hate.
Respect each soul, for God did make.

A nation mourns for all who died.
Let justice forever be our guide.

We honor all who heed the call
to give their lives to protect us all.

To those who wear the color blue,
the brave, the honest, and the true.

We lift you up in prayer each day.
May God protect you and keep you safe.

Stand strong, brave souls.
Your march goes on.

Your service, your call to serve
us all.

WATERS SURROUND

Dedicated to the victims of Hurricane Harvey, 2017

Waters surround; misery abounds.
Belongings all gone, but love stands strong.

People of all races and creeds
finding themselves in human need.

All join in to lift one other
as the floodgates of heaven rush over each other.

Sharing the same space,
never noticing race.

All together.

All displaced.

What comes next, no one knows.
Waters rush in; time flows.

Human suffering sure to come.
Joining in to become one.

On this earth as waters flow,
and ruin the life that we once did know.

All is not lost, though it may seem—
mankind at its best, a flowing
stream…

GENTLE EYES

Dedicated to the wonderful souls at Life's Adult Day Health Center, Broken Arrow, Oklahoma

Today I saw beauty in gentle eyes.

A man named Hosy, so full of grace,
his beauty shown, all over his face.

I met Hank, once a carpenter,
proud and true;

then Larry, a coach
from a university I knew.

Johnny, a man who loved his late wife.
He loved to talk and share his life.

Ethel, a beauty in pink all aglow,
a gentle, quiet spirit I was proud to know.

Elnora, whose face
told a story all its own.
Beautiful pictures she colored
while sitting alone.

Bonnie, outspoken,
a beautiful voice.

Alice, her first day,
hoping it was the right choice.

Then Bessie, ninety-seven years old,
you see;
she looked like an angel sitting near me.

Virginia, so quiet and shy she could be,
but there was so much more to see.

Mary full of life, vibrant, and free
acting motherly to Tony and me.

Tony, with a laugh,
mischievous, full of glee;
oh, what a kidder he can be.

Michelle, happy and content
as she embroidered.

And Pearl, the wise and gentle one,
observant and kind, encouraging me.

We talked, we ate,
we sang, and we listened.

When I left,
my heart, was on a mission

to show God's love to each one I meet,

for He made them, He loves them.
I want them ne'er to forget.

Those gentle eyes, those precious lives,
an honor to know.

May God's grace overflow.

HOSY

———

To my forever friend Hoshang Sorabji Lala (Hosy)
love, "Jo Jo"

My forever friend, you'll always be.
An unlikely friend, for you and me.

Age just a number,
that sets us apart.

But God knew;
you would fill my heart.

Your tender eyes
I'll ne'er forget,

or your sweet and gentle voice
saying "Jo Jo" when we first met.

No one had ever said it
quite that way,

or blessed someone
with such few words to say.

By the time we met,
time had taken its toll.

But never did it stop you
for the world you did show;

that with so little left,
you still gave it your all -

to show The Master's love,
to one and all.

I love you, dear Hosy,
my friend for life.

May God hold you and carry you,
to a better life.

RISING STAR

For Josh

Rising star,
shining bright,

soon the world
will see your light.

Those who know you
love you so.

Soon, others
will also know.

Your God-given talent,
places to go—

let Him guide you,
for He loves you so.

The impact you'll make,
if His path you take,

will be multiplied
as you go.

Be bold and brave,
steadfast and true.

Always let God
carry you through.

As we lift you up in prayer,
we will watch for the light

that God has placed
in you to shine.

Now go fly away, and always come back—
to those who have prayed

for God to use you

in a mighty way.

THE HEART OF A PARENT

For Delsy and Iñaki, after the death of their son, Iñaki, 2010

The heart of a parent,
so amazing, so pure.

Each child that is born
they could love no more.

They say to cherish
each day, each hour,

but time passes by
and, so, the hour.

We love them,
guide them,

stay with them,
take pride in them,

hoping they'll see
the beauty inside them.

One day we look up
only to see

that little one no longer
on our knee.

Our knees bended to Thee,

praying for guidance
and their destiny.

He says that before
we are even formed,

our days are ordained for us
when we are born.

So little may seem
our time on earth,

but eternity He gives us
when in Him we search.

So fear not, dear parents
whose time is lost;

heaven awaits
if in God we believe.

Live your life
full and free,

knowing that God
is waiting for thee.

BABY SONGS

*To my sister Kelly; my brother-in-law Eddie; and all
the moms and dads who missed the baby songs*

There is a sound in heaven's realm
that only babies know,

because on earth they didn't get
to make the sounds we know.

Their little forms may not have been
for moms and dads to hold.

In heaven they make a grand display
we one day will behold.

You see, up there they sit around
the Savior's blessed feet

and make their sounds so beautifully.
They practice at His feet.

One day we'll hear the songs up there
those precious babies make.

And then we'll know why baby sounds—
the Lord He had to take.

RARE GIFTS

To all my precious friends

Rare gifts we gather along the way.
Of the many we gather, not many
will stay.

Each path we travel, each stop we make,
the friends we choose,
our lives will make.

So cleave I will to those rare gifts
who choose to stay
and honor this.

Rare gifts, like jewels
upon the sand,

the *pearls* we seek
to hold in our hands.

GIGGLES AND LAUGHTER

To Melanie, my best friend for life

Giggles and laughter—
friendship ensued.

A bond that life's hardships,
could never undo.

Melanie, my friend for life,
you would be,

the best one I could ever imagine
for me.

Games we played.
Sleepovers abounded.

Trading little treasures
to pass around.

Singing in choir
while at church, we would be;

laughing and talking,
you and me.

What silly little girls
God put together,

a bond forever
that could never be shattered.

Giggles and laughter.
what else could it be?

For you were the one
God meant for me.

THE CAPTAIN

To Brandon and Shaunie
May 2, 2009

Hand in hand
your love began.

Two brought together
by God above

to live in the ocean
of His endless love.

So it is.
But with God, you see,

a companion he gives
to travel the seas.

Stand by each other
through the sands of time,

one hand your companion;
the other, your guide.

For each journey you take,
His light He will shine.

So hold on to Him,
and each other embrace.

Holy and pure,
stand before His face.

WEDDING BELLS

For Michael and Marissa
September 20, 2014

The day has come—
wedding bells will ring.

Marissa and Michael
before the king.

Before His throne
in front of all—

a pledge to love
through it all.

Today you stand
so proud and tall.

To one another
you give your all.

Friends and family,
witnesses to your life.

Together He'll carry you
through the strife.

Treasure all yours,
God has said,

so walk with Him—
your life ahead.

Wedding bells ring;
angels sing.

Each other you have found;
may your love abound.

Dedications

UP ON A HILL

For Chelsea and Steven on their wedding day
May 16, 2015

Up on a hill in front of us all,
Chelsea and Steven heeded a call.

Husband and wife,
a bond made of three;

each of you
and the Master it would be.

With your lives now before you,
don't go it alone.

Your family, a witness,
remain at His throne.

So much in store,
your lives ahead.

Let beauty encompass
the vows you said.

In the days to come
when memories fade,

remember the hill
on which you stayed.

Look up to the heavens
and grab His hand.

Your Father is there,
as He always has been.

LOVE LETTERS
TO FAMILY

IF I COULD LIVE A THOUSAND YEARS

Happy thirtieth anniversary, to my husband,
from the girl who will forever be your Jo

If I could live a thousand years,
I'd give them all to you.

If I could live a thousand years
to make your dreams come true.

The words I'd say, the thoughts I'd share,
would never be enough,

for you, my love, have carried me
through this life so tough.

I'd tell you each and every way
you made me feel so loved.

I'd tell you how your tender touch
was filled with unending love.

Every moment of every day
I'd spend to let you know,

that even with a thousand years,
my words could never show.

So, for today, I'll say the words
that show my love for you:

my Chris, my "pud," my life, my love,
you are my dream come true.

HEROES IN OUR MIDST

To my precious husband

A husband, a wife,
a mother, a friend.

Those untold stories
of *superhero* glories.

Blessed by God
to be the link

between the sufferers,
and the life they so seek.

Often unaware,
the amazing care they give.

One day in glory
they will live,

when God will say,
"Well done, My friend.

You helped one of My
little ones

I put on earth
to teach a lesson

of unconditional love
and abundant blessing.

The link you were
was a mighty task.

And now you are all here
at last!"

THE GOLDEN RING

To "Grandad," the precious father of my dear husband, happy Father's Day

Born in nineteen sixty-three,
a tow-headed boy
the baby would be.

Growing up in a magical land
full of corn and wheat
and God's master plan.

A father so tender,
yet so very strong,
quietly leading his family
along.

Years passed, so full and carefree,
each day an example
of what he would be.

The boy was given a
golden ring,

the gift of a great father
he would someday be.

Now that boy looks back and sees

all he could ask for
and hope to be.

A great father to his child,
he passed *the golden ring.*

TIRELESS HEART

To my mother-in-law, whom I lovingly call "Grandma"

There are those in life who seek no glory,
yet theirs always is a meaningful story.

Going through life putting others first,
no thoughts for themselves, or even their worth.

Always there for every need.
Helping others would be their deed.

I know such a one who fits the part,
a loving mother with a loving heart.

The one who brought up a boy I love,
a man who gives his all, like she has done.

A tireless heart she did impart
to a son and to the world. She left a mark.

So, thank you for the life you gave,
and for the sons and daughter you raised.

Thank you for your *tireless heart*,
the gift you gave—
a loving heart.

BLOND BOY

To my love, on his birthday

Blond-headed boy, youngest of four,
born on a farm in Ashmore.

Frog gigging and fishing, riding tractors
with Dad,

Farming and cattle feeding, camping,
playing tag.

Lighting bugs and critters
all circled round.

Life on the farm,
where love was first found.

Cooking with Mom
while others did go.

Soon too the young blond boy
would come to know.

Life on the farm—
church the front row.

Trusting his Savior,
oh, he did grow.

Learned many lessons
from Bonnie and Bill.

His parents, his role models—
he loves them still.

Raised him up
to be a man of great value.

Married a woman named Jo.
Had a little girl he would know.

So thankful, his wife
treasured parents of the boy,

who had taught him so well
and gave him true joy.

Every tool given, he used for life,
for God and his work, and for loving his wife.

Now looking back—
he is fifty-three.

I wonder who could raise such a boy,
with such glee.

Only one answer
comes to mind:

the names Bonnie and Bill,
forever mine.

Thank you for the man you raised
to be the father he became.

Blond boy so cute,
so full of joy.

Forever my love,

forever
the boy.

KEYS TO MY HEART

To my one true love

You, and you alone,
have the keys to my heart.

Your love sustains me
when I drift too far.

Life with all its joy
and pains.

You hold me, and assure me
it will be the same.

Your love, an everlasting one,
shows me that I picked the one,

the one to hold my heart so near,
to trust my life with, to hold so dear.

It takes you to a place so free,
it shows you who you can be,

when someone treasures you
like you do me.

I blossom into
who I was meant to be.

So here I give you
the only key,

for you are my
eternity.

MY WARRIOR VALENTINE

From your Valentine

When I have no words
and I have no will,

I see God's mighty hands
working still.

I see Him clearly
in the man I love,

the *beautiful one*
sent from above.

I see a reflection
of what a husband should be

in the man
God gave to me.

A tireless warrior on every front,
fighting battles on behalf of all he loves.

His family in high esteem he holds,
protecting them valiantly as he goes.

I see a warrior in you,
my Valentine,

a fearless man of integrity,

a man of honor, a man of God.

My warrior Valentine,

my all in all.

CASEY'S POEM

Small, I came into the world
a tiny two-pound
baby.

A miracle, I was told.

My life would soon
unfold.

A blessing for my parents,

so adored.

They said I was a special gift

from the Lord.

A complete family made up of three.

My name would be
Casey Marie.

Life so blessed;
who could ask for more?

Healthy and strong,
now I can
soar

to be whatever God intends.
I will wait for whatever

He sends.

Written by Casey and Jo

OCEANS DEEP AND OCEANS WIDE

To Casey, our tiny two-pound baby!

Oceans deep, or oceans wide
could not contain our love inside.

Our little girl born so small,
our cherished treasure through it all.

A gift so precious, ours to receive.
God must have known we were on our knees.

Praising God for each breath you took,
each time you moved, and every look.

The greatest peace we've ever known
during the early times of unknown.

While others feared,
we carried on

for you were our wish
all along.

OUR LETTER TO CASEY

To Casey on her high school graduation

The day came too quickly,
the years went by too fast.
Each moment we prayed
would last and last.

Trying to remember
what wise ones, had said
to cherish every moment
that we would have.

So, we did. We listened,
and never let slip by
a laugh, a look,
a silly goodbye.

Each year you blossomed
like a beautiful tree.
Each moment we held,
each memory.

Now we have reached
the day when we will see,
our beautiful Casey
too amazing to believe.

God gave us our dream of
the perfect three,

you, me, and your dad
it would be.

Now go out into God's world
and never be afraid,
for when he made you,
there was no mistake.

Be who God
has designed you to be,
and keep growing like
a beautiful tree.

Now we share you
with a world in need

of beauty and hope
and tranquility.

Just be the person
we know you to be.

Let your Father in heaven
be the guide for thee.

The rest of your life
has just begun.

Cherish each moment
as we have done.

THAT'S WHAT YOU ARE

To my Casey, with love

Irreplaceable, chosen, and treasured,

that's what you are.

Beautiful, priceless, and precious,

that's what you are.

Valued, dependable, bright,

that's what you are.

Brave, silly, and talented,

that's what you are.

God's little miracle,

That's who you are.

Favored by God,

That's who you are.

"...Fearfully and wonderfully made"
(Psalms 139:14 KJV)

that's who you are.

THE SUN AND THE MOON AND THE STARS

To Casey on her college graduation

The sun and the moon and the stars—
that's what you are.

A pearl in the shell
on the sparkling glittery sand.

A priceless treasure in the sea—
no one else could ever be.

The most fragrant flower
in a field

growing and yielding
life surreal.

Oceans deep and oceans wide
could not contain our love inside.

A lifetime of searching
could never reveal

the joy you've brought,
the lives you've filled.

Put here on earth,
so loved from birth,

God's precious gift
from above.

A cherished baby so delicate but strong.

God's masterful creation,

His love, beyond—

anything we could have ever imagined,
or for which we could have ever longed.

Now we release you.
His plan evolves.

So proud, so amazed.
A graduate you've become.

The sun, and the moon, and the stars
all in one.

"RING, RING" GO THE BELLS

To Casey and Josh on their wedding day
May 5, 2018

"Ring, ring" go the bells.
The day has come; time will tell.

Soon we'll give away the bride!
Mom and Dad so full of pride.

The one she has chosen to hold her heart.
Few have hastened to ever start.

The jewel we have raised from a tiny stone
has grown so big, it must ne'er be alone.

Letting go of such a precious one
cannot be done by us alone.

So, take her now, to hold and to love,
always reminding her
of God's
great love.

This tiny baby we once held—
now rests in your arms, so hold her well.

Nearer to God, then nearer to you,
this precious stone, always new.

"Ring, ring" go the bells.
Casey and Josh, a fairy tale!

IF BY WORDS

For my Mom, following Casey's high school graduation

If by words the gratitude
of the heart.

If by words we could hug
and ne'er part.

If by words one could tell you
how much you are loved.

The miles apart
would be only be a shrug.

If by words one could say
"Thank you for a heart so full,

because all of life,
has been what it should."

The daughter you raised
now understands,

what pain and sorrow
and braveness it took,

to let go of a child
and show her to love,

so one day she could know
the lessons of letting go.

Hard lessons to learn,
but even so, we must.

Those moments secured
in a *mother's heart*

always return
and never depart.

If by words
I could tell you what joy I feel

and replace all the sadness
that love, always heals,

I would say, "Thank you,
sweet Mother,
for all you have done.

The jewels in your crown
will be many, not one."

OUR FIRST LOVE

For my Mom on Valentine's Day 2011

The one who held me first.
The one who kissed my cheeks.

My tiny eyes glistening
as she stood by listening.

Each sound,
such a joy to behold.

Another baby girl.
"We'll call this one
Jo."

Jo grew up to be silly
and strong.

always knowing
she belonged

to a mom who loves her
like no one else does.

Although not always the case,
yet in this it is true.

So grateful a girl
could have a mom like you—

with a heart full of love,
growing each day.

Our first love we cherish
on this Valentine's Day.

I love you, sweet Mom.
I pray you know,

for you see, our first love
will never go.

BEAUTIFUL ONE

For your birthday, Mom

Beautiful one, love of my heart,
when you were born, the stars did part.

A child so beautiful, so precious, and so loved
sent from the Lord up above.

Wish I had known you as a child back then,
so prissy and delicate, like a gentle wind.

I would have taken you by the hand
and told you for life, I'd be your friend.

I would have loved and protected you—
so fierce I would be,

so no one could harm
my "little thee."

God had a plan for us to meet, not as a friend
but a daughter you'd need—

to hold you and love you
for life it would be.

So happy birthday, my mom,
my "little thee."

May God look down upon you,
and blessings you'll see.

MOM

For my dear mom

Your strength shines bright
through God's pure light.

Tho' tiring and wearying
your road has been,

God's promises
will never end.

He sees your pain;
He knows your heart.

He will not leave you,
nor depart.

A new journey
you must take.

But we know
'tis no mistake.

On His promises, His truths,
we must rely.

With these our hope
may never die.

Let others carry you,
tho' hard it may be.

The Master sent others
to watch over thee.

Soon it will be over.
God's grace you shall see.

He will now and always
watch over thee.

NEVER UNNOTICED

My dad, my hero
ever you'll be,

the one whose strength
I did always see.

Seesaws and go-carts,
rides on the mower.

Lessons learned,
games played.

A child's wish
of no more.

A magical childhood,
magical time.

Safe in Daddy's arms,
your love all mine.

Always seeking
to see that *smile*.

That brightened my day,
if only for a while.

My dad, my hero
forever you'll be,

the one I know
who has cherished me.

May God bless you, sweet father,
and give you peace,

knowing that on this earth,
as heaven did see

a Fathers' love,
a hero to me

never unnoticed,
for I love thee.

BYE, BUDDY

To my Dad on his eightieth birthday

Words of a father to his child,
words I've cherished for a while.

Softly spoken, simple and pure,
him patiently waiting to reassure.

Conversations with my dad,
cherished beyond measure.

Forever I have.

Each day I pray you know the love
I have for you, so far above

what earthly words can ne'er express.
My love for you, dear Dad, so blessed.

For all the years you've given to me,
I ask the Lord to bless thee.

Each time we talk, I wait to hear
"bye, buddy," the words I hold so dear.

Wait I will, each and every day,
so on another birthday I can say:

"Dear Dad, I love you so—

God hold you, and bless you,
from
your Jo."

THREE SISTERS

To my beautiful sisters. I'll love you forever.

Three sisters. The number—
how perfect could it be?

Two extra buddies with *life* to see—

playtime dress-up, matching,
all three.

Sisters, sisters,
how blessed we would be.

Someone to call, someone to pray,
someone to wipe the tears away.

A lifelong gift.

A treasure times three.

Sisters, sisters—one, two, three.

Kelly, Karla, Jo,

the perfect three.

TEN YEARS OLD

To my precious brothers, Ronnie and Bobby

Ten years old,
thoughts sublime.
Long-haired girl; life was fine.

News so exciting:
twin brothers are here!

Couldn't wait to hold them near.

Dress them up,
feed them bottles,

watch them grow
at full throttle.

Life not the same.
these boys that I love,

mischievous, silly, and fun to hug.

Now all grown up.
I love them so.

They've shown me how
my heart could grow.

Long-haired girl;
life was fine.

Two brothers—yes, twins.
My life *sublime*.

ANGEL ON EARTH

To my beautiful nanna and paw paw

Nana,
the name that means so much.

Her lovely hands,
her soft touch.

The sweet-spoken words
of an angel on earth.

This was my nana,
whom I knew from birth.

A kind and gentle spirit,
like a flower in spring.

I know that when she spoke,
angels did sing.

It wasn't for naught
God put her here.

The lives she touched,
He holds so dear.

For when someone is born,
who holds such gifts

as my nana did,
we will always miss.

I miss the way you looked at me,
the way you held me on your knees.

I miss your words
and godly advice.

I miss your corn bread
and pumpkin pie.

I miss your creamed corn.
You know why!

I miss the love I felt inside.
I miss the hugs you would provide.

So, as I go along my way,
I say, "Dear Nana
for you I'll stay!

I'll stay upon the earth awhile.
Please tell Paw Paw that I miss his smile."

I miss how he enjoyed
our laughter.

I'll miss him always,
until the hereafter.

So, here's a kiss and a hug for you,
my *angel* who always saw me through.

GRANNY AND PAW PAW

To my granny and paw paw. I miss you.

Dear, dear Granny,
I want to say

Paw Paw and you;
I miss this day,

I miss the farm, the family times
chasing the peacocks, living the farm life.

Looking for kittens in the barn,
running around on your farm.

The family dinners;
a feast for all.

We gathered around
our dear paw paw.

I'll ne'er forget the memories,
the times we shared our family.

Thank you for those moments in time.
I'll always cherish them, and remind;

remind the others down the line

how the Bryson family
was designed.

A legacy you left behind.

"FUZZY MAN"

To my great-uncle Edgerton, whom we lovingly called
"Fuzzy Man" when funny, we couldn't pronounce

There was a man named "Fuzzy Man"

whom all the world should know.

Although my memory fails me some,
I want the world to know—

the part he played in my life,
the *funnies* he bestowed.

Who was this man called "Fuzzy Man",
the one I'll always know,

the one who brought the smiles to us?

The family loves him so ...

TOMMY AND LYNN, SITTING IN A TREE

*To my uncle Tommy and to my family whom I love
dearly, on the occasion of Tommy's tragic death
July 30, 2017*

Rhymes of youth, so young and free,
words remembered of a life to be.

Forty-eight years, children sublime,
hunting, fishing, growing a family line.

Beautiful grandchildren and daughters-in-law

wanting to take part in it all.

A loving community;
The Brysons would be,

part of a long
history.

Generations of faith,
passed on through time,

never forgotten
never to unwind.

Country life, so
charmed, so free,

but not without pain,
so one stays on one's knees.

Generations of ties
by pain unbroken.

Brought together for love—
which was not *shaken!*

No evil could tarnish
the Bryson name

when one of their loved ones
was *taken*, not *claimed!*

Heaven cried tears on those to blame,
as one of its own He knew by name.

But still the glory of God was shown,

though the family suffered the loss of *Tom.*

The life shortened by earthly sin
shines bright in heaven, for all to win.

To win the heart of God so true,
we must let others see us through.

Then on that glorious day, we'll wait

in heaven, we'll meet
at the pearly white gate!

NEW BEGINNINGS

To my suffering family after Tommy's death

When life appears, it will never be the same,
look up to Him and call on His name.

Tell Him of your sorrows,
your worries and fears.

Let Him surround you
and carry your tears.

Tears that flow so freely so vast,
only His hand can hold at last.

Open your heart and tears will flow –
in time the spout, will gently close.

For each time a tear falls from your face,
the God of mercy will give you grace.

He gives you grace
and sets you free,

like a fawn jumping o'er
the leaves in spring.

New beginnings
lie ahead.

Now lay down
your weary head.

FANTASTICAL

ELSA, ELSA, MY MALTIPOO

From your mama and papa

Elsa, Elsa, my Maltipoo,
dreams and wishes do come true.
Curiosity, naughtiness, running through
this silly little Maltipoo.

Praying for God to send a pup,
never knowing how much we'd be up!

Emergency room visits,
nerves on end.

Little tiny Elsa
just wouldn't bend.

Keeps us going, night and day,
intrigued, and laughing, along the way.

Never know what will happen next
with this tiny Maltese mix.

Great things in small packages do come,
but in this case, even less than one.

Keeps us on our toes.
Taught her a trick: *to nose!*

Darling little Elsa, our Maltipoo,
better than having Winnie the Pooh!

Fantastical

JASMINE AND LUCE

From your loving family, for all you gave

Jasmine and Luce, a dream come true.
A life well spent, a life of two.

Two precious Maltese we had to release,
but years they gave before they were deceased.

To the family they loved,
they did add such joy.

What more could we have asked
from these girls, not boys?

Born to fill our home with love,
two little Maltese sent from above.

We loved you both, tiny white charms.
We loved to carry you in our arms.

Jasmine and Luce,
our little Maltese,

we'll see you in heaven,
when we are released!

I THOUGHT I'D SIT AWHILE TODAY

I thought I'd sit awhile today
and ponder life the regular way.

I thought of things that should be done,
but as I sat, I thought of none.

I stood awhile and thought some more,
but then my mind wandered more.

I thought of how the country roads
lead to things only animals know.

I thought that if I were a rabbit,
I'd be developing quite a habit.

I would jump and jump
as high as I could.

I'd hop over fences;
I'd hop over hoods.

I'd hop into shopping carts,
and off I would go.

And then I might
take a boat, and row.

I'd row in the water;
I'd catch me some fish.

I'd put on some sunscreen
and look like a dish!

Cuter and cuter
I would become,

Till all the other bunnies
would see me, and run!

So as I sat for a while today,
and pondered bunnies going astray,

I realized after a day like today
that being a bunny, I was not to stay.

TODAY I WALKED AMONG THE CLOUDS

Today I walked among the clouds
and saw a curious thing.

I stood and stared and wondered there.
My eyes could ne'er believe.

Before my eyes I saw it there,
a sight I'd never seen,

a tiny baby crocodile
sitting on a swing!

I thought and thought to myself,
What could she be doing?

But as I stared some more, you see,
she wasn't in my viewing.

INSPIRATIONAL

TEARS

As tears roll across my face,
I count them not as loss.

For every one that falls, I know
the Savior knows them all.

He cares for each and every one.
The weight of each He knows.

Through the pain that makes them fall,
His love to us He shows.

So as the tears flow down, dear one,
don't hold them back today.

Each one has meaning; it cleanses us
to show us and convey—

that as they come upon our face,
He will not let us stay;

alone with them for very long—
the Shepherd shows the way.

BLESSINGS

Tonight I count my blessings.
Tonight I say my prayers.

I thank my God, my Savior,
for all I hold so dear.

The earth, the moon,
the stars so bright;

the world He holds
in His arms so tight.

For giving me a family,
that means so very much to me.

For food and shelter,
for joy and peace,

through life's hard journey.
His presence I will keep.

Tonight I count my blessings;
I count them one by one.

For all we have and hope for,

God sent us

His Son.

CHILDHOOD PRAYERS

Childhood prayers,
so innocent and free.

No hint of obscurity.

A prayer meant
for God alone.

So precious and trusting
His love, our own.

For if we could pray
with childlike faith,

what joy and peace
we would obtain.

For God knows our hearts
before we speak,

so pray like a child,
and in Him, believe,

that when we pray,
we will receive.

WHAT CAN I GIVE?

To my Father in heaven

So what can I give
to You, my Lord?

My life, sometimes empty
and ignored.

Desiring to be all
You want me to be,

I seek Your face
while on my knees.

I want my life
to count for You,

here on earth
and in glory too.

Teach me Your will
and I will obey.

For each step I take,
You will show me the way.

Help me to rely
only on You,

not on myself,
to see me through.

I desire to live
a life worthy of You.

So show me, dear Lord.
I want to be
renewed.

MYSTERY

God gives us one life
here on earth,

to do his will
from our birth.

Some choose their own path
and succeed for a while.

Living for oneself
is not His desire.

Life's mystery
is to share Him with others.

And in doing so,
each man, becomes

our brother.

ONE PATH

A world so confused,
trying this and that.

If they only understood
there is just one path.

One path
to the God of creation,

one path
for our nation.

Other religions
claim to be

the way, if only
one believes.

Look at His Word.
The history

of one God, one way
it is not a mystery!

Soon all will know
the truth revealed.

God, in His mighty power,
will not yield!

The earth is His,
and all will see

one triumphant day,
when it all

will be …

ONE LIFE

We have one life
with which to give,

each one so precious
yet oft unlived.

Caught up in fears,
doubts, and confusion,

when will we learn
it is all an *illusion*?

This world cannot offer
what it is we seek.

Only He who made us
can make us complete.

There is no illusion;
He has made it clear.

Life is about serving others
and bringing them

to Him.

WAKE UP

Wake up, o weary souls on earth,
let music bellow round!

Give birth. The day sneaks in to warm
the light; the glory surrounds.

Each burst of light a different hue.
Soon the sky gives way.

Break free from yesterday's mistakes.
Start new. Look upon His face.

Music strums, the strings in tune.
The day awaits; do not loom.

Waste not another moment, instead—

turn to Him.

Lift up your head!

GOD OF THE OCEANS

To my mighty God and Savior
Written on the day of the total solar eclipse, 2017

God of the oceans, God of the seas,

the world that You have given is our pleasure to see.

A world so vast, no man can undo.

A lifetime of searching through and through.

No one can compare the love you have cast,

a brilliant radiance, a love unsurpassed.

God of the oceans, God of the seas,

You created it all

for the world
to see.

Inspirational

ABOUT THE AUTHOR

Karen "Jo" Weber lives in Oklahoma, with her devoted husband, Chris, her amazing and beautiful daughter, Casey, and a, mischievous Maltipoo, named Elsa.

She grew up in Etowah, North Carolina, where she lived a magical childhood. It was at Etowah Baptist Church, where she gave her life to Christ Jesus, at the age of eight. Through the many challenges and trials of life, she learned many lessons. She learned that even with almost four decades of chronic pain and numerous health problems, that her Savior has been by her side - crying with her, mourning with her, and holding her up, when she did not feel she could bear any more. The bible says, "You keep track of all my sorrows. You have collected all my tears in your bottle. You have recorded each one in your book." (Ps 56:8, NLT) As she grows in Christ, she is forever touched by His compassion for her, and his prodding her to never give up, to share

His love with others, and, "to fight the good fight of faith." (1 Tim 6:12, NIV)

Although not all her poems are inspirational, her goal in life is to always magnify the Lord and inspire others.

Printed in the United States
By Bookmasters